LIVING YOUR
BIGGER STORY

LIVING YOUR BIGGER STORY

⊂◦⊃

THE PRACTICE OF SELF-REMEMBRANCE

JACQUELYN SMALL

A Hazelden Book
HarperCollins*Publishers*

LIVING YOUR BIGGER STORY:
The Practice of Self-Rememberance.

FIRST HARPERCOLLINS PAPERBACK EDITION PUBLISHED IN 1995

———————————

Library of Congress Cataloging-in-Publication Data
ISBN 0-06-255275-9 (pbk. : alk. paper)

———————————

95 96 97 98 99 HAD 10 9 8 7 6 5 4 3 2 1

This edition is printed on acid-free paper that meets
the American National Standards Institute Z39.48 Standard.

INTRODUCTION

STEPPING INTO YOUR GREATER IDENTITY

What, on a lower level, had led to the wildest conflicts and to panicky outbursts of emotion, now looks like a storm in the valley seen from the mountain top. This does not mean that the storm is robbed of its reality, but instead of being in it, one is above it.

—CARL GUSTAV JUNG
ALCHEMICAL STUDIES

There's a bigger You who is your constant companion and who sees the overview. This "Observer" Self is who you really are, a wise Self who can think clearly beyond all the twists and turns you travel in your ordinary life. We've not been taught much about this inner Knower who can hold the vision, even in the midst of your "wildest conflicts and panicky outbursts." This part of you feels compassion for all Humanity, so Its motivations are always pure and harmless. It is a Fair Witness consciousness, keyed to your greater life that's unfolding on a larger canvas. This Self never leaves you.

Your true Self's function is to nudge you gently back onto your path anytime you lose touch with your highest intentions. You can fulfill your purpose here now, for our time of completion has come. Humanity is about to move into a whole new consciousness. But as we end this millennium and begin a whole new era of human history, many are still sleeping, not the least prepared for this awesome event!

We've all spent time looking back at who we've been. But unfortunately, when we constantly view ourselves through a rearview mirror, we lose touch with our potential. We don't have an image of our greater Identity. Instead, we're constantly reacting to our past, and this distorts our present interactions. Oprah Winfrey once said, "We all see now that we're from dysfunctional homes. So what are we going to do about it?" Most people haven't yet realized that we need to turn in a whole new direction to move ahead. *We are the meaning makers of our lives.* Whatever we focus on and give meaning to becomes our reality.

Mythologist Joseph Campbell said that we'd better have a great big story, or no story at all. It's getting caught up in those middle-sized stories that causes so much trouble. When you can see your Bigger Story through a wider lens, you become conscious of larger patterns and storylines that may have kept you hooked into your past.

You might think of this book as your instruction guide for turning inward and reconnecting with your *real* Story, the one that's unfolding in the much larger framework of your subjective inner life. It's here in this "soul-sized" life that your true ideals take shape.

To move beyond where you are, you'll need a new definition for yourself. Little has been taught to us, however, about our *greater* side, this magnificent potential Self. This One represents your highest expression as a soul in human form. Certainly worthy of your recognition, wouldn't you say?

Your greater Self wills your actions through two main qualities, Wisdom and Love. What you *think* with your Mind and *feel* in your Heart is ultimately who you become. Jesus said, "As a man thinketh in his heart, so is he."

As you read, you'll become reacquainted with these two aspects of your nature that are living through you from inside. And, perhaps, if you are somewhat out of balance here—too cerebral and detached, or too emotional and attached—you may find yourself more balanced. For the Middle Way is the key to peace of mind. It's from the midpoint, not the extremes, that we learn to be *in the world, but not of it.*

Your Bigger Story is part of a Divine Plan; therefore, it has archetypal significance. Archetypes are Humanity's Divine Ideals. These are the blueprints we're growing into. When your time of completion comes, you'll blossom fully into your whole design.

Our main task, then, while in human form is to be forever willing to interpret our life story within its greater sacred Purpose. Then we'll take on our true spiritual identities.

In terms of seeing this bigger picture, the great philosopher Arthur Schopenhauer made this analogy:*

*Bailey Saunders, trans., *Essays from Parergra and Paralipomena* (London, 1951).

Life may be compared to a piece of embroidery of which, during the first half of our time, we get a sight of the right side, and during the second half, of the wrong. The wrong side is not as pretty . . . but it is more instructive; it shows the way in which the threads have been worked together [to make the pattern].

In these pages you'll meet your most reliable Guides for showing you the wrong side of your tapestry, your wise inner Knower and your compassionate Heart. Your Divine Ideals hold the key.

All of Humanity is passing through a threshold now into a new dimension. This will require a shift in our *perspective*—a transformation in mind. Once we understand, we can do this in the twinkling of an eye. When your identity is with these Higher

Principles, you'll feel inspired with Spiritual Intent. You will claim your full powers as a human soul and be able to rise quite effortlessly to the next place in your evolution. This new One you're becoming is moving into an entirely different world, a world in harmony. And you may be one of those who are choosing to wake up and go first. But before you can transcend your old Self, you must recognize the principles of your Higher Life with an attitude of complete sincerity and willingness to do your part. You must abide by certain rules of the road. Your sincerity and willingness are *powers* that bring you closer to your highest Spiritual Intentions. Use these well, and you will evolve rapidly along this accelerated path, familiar to the mystics of every age. When you can function more from the Higher Principles, all else falls into place.

To *consciously* choose to evolve sets you apart. All of nature is evolving, of course, but most people just allow nature to take its course, not really wanting to take on spiritually evolving as a conscious activity. You can feel this resistance in many people, maybe in some of the people closest to you; it's even in society's institutions. If you choose this more accelerated path, you won't be in the majority; but you will make the new Life a Reality—so your mission is sacred. It is a vital function for Humanity as a whole.

You'll find a transformational journey is not for the fainthearted! Inviting your whole Self into your conscious life changes you—forever. It brings you from unconscious to conscious living. Be sure you're willing, for you may never again look at your life in the same old familiar way. Your Higher Mind and Heart will bring a whole new perspective to your personal life.

I hope what follows validates what you already instinctively know in the depths of your soul and gives you exactly what you need to make your transformation.

GREAT CHANGES ARE IN STORE!

It is the worst thing when people do not know how to escape from the old rut. It is dreadful when they approach new conditions with their old habits. Just as it is impossible to open a present-day lock with a medieval key, likewise it is impossible for people with old habits to unlock the door of the future.

—AGNI YOGA TEACHINGS
INFINITY, VOL. II

We look around us and see that much of what we've always taken for granted is shape-shifting before our very eyes. Much dogma that had stuck to us like glue, beliefs we'd bought into because "they" said so, is peeling off our frozen minds and crumbling into ash, along with many of our taken-for-granted idols and ideals. Our identities are smashing against walls we can't make it through as fragmented selves. A great many people are expressing discontent with their lives:

- I want to live more simply so I can pursue my real life's work.
- More money doesn't do it for me anymore.
- I feel like my life force is drying up.
- Everything just fell apart while I was going merrily along. But it seems to be some kind of gift.

- Another great lesson is resolved, and now I'm moving on.

These are statements I've heard lately. Some people believe the critical mass that shapes Humanity has come and we're all about to change. There is a search for personal meaning and fulfillment within the human soul, and it's right out there where everyone can see.

In the midst of outer confusion and disillusionment, you may be hearing an inner call to awaken and live more attuned to the real essentials in your life. There's an urgency to align with something greater than we are, or we sense we may not even survive.

We've believed all along that we were just living our lives. Our robotlike day-in, day-out routines make it seem this way. But now, we may sense that *a Greater Life just might be living us!*

We make up this co-creative process as we go along. For *we are Self-Evolving organisms!* There is an old story that tells of the "wingless bird" who is stuck in Humanity's conditions. It has been trapped in its plight for so long that it has forgotten how to fly. At some point, a "winged bird" with visionary powers arrives and attaches itself to this wingless bird, merging with it and leading it back to freedom. This ability to merge with something higher is the same for us. This is transcendence.

The perennial philosophy describes this movement up the evolutionary ladder as "the spiritual history of the soul's unfolding life into the cosmic flow." Metaphysics, astronomy, archeology, astrophysics, cosmology, spiritual psychology, and the mystical paths of both the East and the West all teach of this greater life. They call it the "science of the soul." You become part of this greater life as you learn to demonstrate divine principles. Our own direct knowledge is a "scientific library" of the bigger, *soul-sized* facts that can steady us while our egos "die."

A new millennium is dawning. A new way of knowing our God-nature is being revealed to us right now. In this passing age we learned devotion and how to worship a transcendent outer God. Now we're turning inward and learning of the immanent God, the "God-within" all of nature, including our own. When we recognize that the God-force lives inside our own nature, we become capable of masterful expression. This is a transformative insight, but it's also a huge responsibility.

First we must resolve our psychological issues. We need to make the emotional distortions that rule our spiritual lives conscious before we can assume our real spiritual identities.

This is where the Observer Self comes in. This Observer part of us is not caught up in the chaos of our emotional lives; it sees the bigger picture. Understanding our experiences through the larger context of each predicament we face, we begin to build inner strength.

The Observer Self is not just a subjective psychological reality, however; it is a scientific fact. Modern physics has discovered that until we make an observation, our consciousness is not attracted to anything and does not create anything. Everything stays in the background, an undifferentiated field of movement and energy. Science has concluded that there is no reality except what we choose to observe and call "real." Physicist Fred Alan Wolf says the manner in which we perceive things is determining our lives. "The how of it determines the what of it," says Wolf.*

*Richard Leviton, "Through the Shaman's Doorway," *Yoga Journal* (July/August 1992).

⚮

Participating Consciously in Your Own Creation

We can see from the "bird's-eye view" that renewal is our constant activity, that is, if we are willing to accept life's challenges with an adventuresome spirit, willing to become involved in whatever crosses our path with integrity.

Your soul-making process naturally unfolds within you as sequences of dying to the lesser life to make room for the greater One that is always evolving. This is not *physical* death; it is a constant flow through life, dying to the old and being reborn to the new, all in this one body!

Some rebirths are small, when we've died to something fairly insignificant, like letting go of something that just wasn't very important to us—a relationship, a possession, an idea. Others, however, can be huge and may even require professional help. For example, we might experience the death of a major role or aspect of our life we felt we needed—something like the loss of a significant relationship that nurtured us or the job that gave us our financial support.

This unrelenting movement toward wholeness is the workings of a human "individuation" that culminates in our blossoming into completion. The great psychologist Carl Gustav Jung spent most of his life studying and writing about this process. To *individuate* means "to become an indivisible whole, no longer capable of being divided." This process is universal. It's how we humans move from fragmentation to wholeness. It is the work of "soul-making," the shift from being ego-dominated to allowing a greater spiritual identity to come in and spontaneously guide your life. Can you imagine yourself as completely dominated by the urges of your soul, no longer needy as an ego? Think about it for a minute. What image do you see?

Moving into greater and greater identity through the process of individuation is to move perpetually in the direction of more and more freedom. If we choose to develop consciously, we continue to attract new possibilities that enrich our lives. If we remain unconscious participators in life, however, we tend to attract the same old lessons to ourselves, *ad nauseam!* The actors or the costumes may change, even the geography, but the issues remain unchanged and we do not evolve or grow.

For each of us, and for Humanity as a whole, individuation is the soul's maturation. This maturation maximizes each of our unique personalities and eventually each of us merges back into the archetypal Self, Humanity as one Soul. From the Self we originate, and to the Self we return when complete.

Before going any further in your Self-exploration, stop for a moment and reflect on how you identify yourself. Who do you *think* you are? If I were to ask you right now, "Who are you?" what would you reply? For a great Self-awareness exercise, stop right now and write down ten endings to the phrase "I am . . ."

Now take some time to reflect on how you are using these magical words, "I am." What are you applying your entire identity to?

This question of identity is a serious issue, ruling your entire life. Whatever we become identified with will dominate us, and whatever we can dis-identify from, we can direct and use. Before we can ever become whole or healed, we must be clear on exactly who we believe we are and what we believe we are here for. Otherwise, none of it has meaning. We'll live as egos, only looking outward to others for our identities. We'll buy into each illusion that appeals to us as of the moment—to have the ideal lover, the career that pays well financially, the perfect vacation. This misses the point of our incarnation story, which is a very "high" story indeed, rich with meaning and sacred Purpose.

We've been preoccupied, busily wrapped up in our ego selves. We're entrenched in our own storylines, not even knowing they are part of something much greater. It is as though we've been enchanted, just like in a fairy tale.

The Self, our soul, is our essence. Our original individuation took place when we were first a divine Idea from God. Next, we individuated biologically, from the body of our mothers. Later, we individuate psychologically, claiming our own needs and interests. And finally, we emerge as our real Selves to consciously serve the whole. Many of us get stalled along the way with leftovers from the prior stage, no longer useful and contaminating our current purpose.

Our central core is a spark of the Divine. Most people, however, haven't yet consciously had a direct experience of God or of their numinous nature. Though these sacred experiences are unfolding within our subjective lives on a regular basis, many will discount them as being figments of the imagination. They do not yet realize their outer lives are only a reflection of a much greater Life, the archetypal process that "lives us" from our inner nature. Many are still looking outward for their identities. We must use the bird's-eye view to bring our potential wholeness into focus. The wingless bird cannot see it.

So now you know: the Self is *not* the ego! Make this distinction right now. The Self *dons* the ego so it can identify with society and relate to the status quo—so it can fit in well enough to do its sacred work. The ego is only your outer shell, the one who takes all the grief! Your ego is your soul's personality, the mask created so your soul could take on human form.

The egos of people who know nothing of the Self are defensive and fearful. When the ego is wounded, it behaves irrationally. It projects its emotionality onto others. Fear is very understandable since people who don't know the Self are not aware of their center.

Anytime we function, even for a moment, as this whole Self, we get a deep sense of well-being, sometimes even a peak experience. These unexplainable, non-ordinary events happen occasionally to many people. In fact, a poll indicated that over 70 percent of Americans claim to have had at least one mystical experience. We call these encounters with the Self "non-ordinary." Isn't this a shame? Why couldn't our identity as this real Self be our "ordinary" experience? Well, it can, and I'll show you how. But I must warn you, be sure that you are willing and sincere. In our work we say, "Let Reality govern my every thought, and Truth be the Master of my life." We've learned that this means all untruth in our life falls away. Dying to our illusions is accompanied by sorrow and pain. But we also say good-bye to them with a certain sigh of relief, for our illusions, though they die hard, are usually troublesome for our evolving soul.

How the Self "Works Us" and Transforms Our Nature

To shift to the God-within, we encounter archetypes and all our subjective realities, for our inner nature is not physical—it is psychic! It is our subjective life and therefore personal. Our God-within is personal as well. We can access the God-within through our minds and hearts.

Like the organs in our physical body, each archetype functions in our psyches to bring a pure quality to fruition or to dismantle an illusion that's blocking our growth. Archetypes personify our abstract Self and build mental images of our ideals. We must have an image of something in our minds before it can be created. This psychological law explains sayings like "Thought is creative" and "Energy follows thought."

Archetypal influences function just like instincts in our psychic life; they act on our subconscious the same way our human instincts act on us biologically. Just as we automatically react when we encounter danger, we also have automatic psychodynamic reactions. We even feel them in our bodies. For instance, we may be overly reactive to mild criticism if we've never integrated the archetype for Power. Spontaneous reactions come upon us like fate when we are under their influence.

When we focus on any specific archetype, activating it in our lives, it becomes a transformer. Mythical motifs are archetypal, the perfect Lover, the ideal Warrior, an act of Courage, the classic

Betrayal, and so on. Processes can also be archetypal, like Death, Birth, and Transformation. These are experienced universally by every human, regardless of which culture they came from originally. Higher Mind, Observer Self, Heart, the Self— these are pure expressions of our Divine Essence, and they are all key players in our Divine unfolding. Higher Mind is the one we'll learn about here. But you can make any one of them your Guide whenever the situation calls for the special traits inherent in some archetype. Your Self wears many faces in its archetypal dimension, just as your ego behaves as various people at different times.

It's important to remember at all times that the archetypes have *archetypal nature only,* not physical nature. We don't actually identify as an archetype; we absorb its characteristics, own and recognize its influence on our consciousness. We only know archetypes, in fact, by their powerful impulses and their imprints upon our lives.

Archetypal interplay is very active during certain cycles in our lives when transformation is necessary. The archetype's function is to bring on a powerful crisis of some kind—to focus us on a higher level of consciousness, where everything is symbolic.

Unfortunately, we're usually only aware of the more newsworthy events of our world, so we see more of archetypal negativity than we do grand acts of courage or reverence for life that Humanity also brings forth. We must also keep these higher aspects of our nature in mind while we pass through Humanity's "dark night."

The archetype of the Self is the One who observes from on high, and when active, affects us on every level of consciousness, leaving no part of our old identity untouched. This is why we must learn to use our Observer Self as a daily spiritual practice—so its archetypal function can enlighten us about all our actions and reactions. All of us are making *all* of Humanity's issues conscious at the close of this millennium. Our Observer Self will bring us closer to our completion.

The key to our freedom is for each of us to do our part in this co-creative process—and commit to heal ourselves and focus on the highest good. At the top of the next page is the magic formula for success.

*First, we must **observe**; second, change our course to refocus on what we spiritually **intend**. These are the powers of **Sincerity** and **Willingness** in action. Then, the rest moves ahead on its own; the rest is Higher Power's "part."*

Your real Self continually guides you through intuitive hunches, deep insights, or revelations—those "ahas!" that come from out of the blue that you know are inspired. The Self is the One who creates the content of your dreams, either when you are awake or asleep. If you have spontaneous dreams, with content you didn't create with your ego brain, you must realize some kind of Grand Designer is at work.

CO

Take a moment now to reflect on a period in your life when you went through a powerful transformative experience—a time when you sensed that Destiny had a strong influence on your life. . . . Once you recall this time, try to remember the quality or trait at the core of the experience. Recall the feelings that led up to this event. . . .

What was *really* going on at the archetypal level during this intense time? Observe this from your Higher Mind. Let the Image or Idea behind the experience emerge. . . . Once you capture this in your mind, you've discovered the archetypal process that was represented. This can lead you to see the larger pattern for this aspect of your individuation.

So now you're becoming conscious of how to use your Higher Mind. Whatever the mind believes is real will eventually manifest itself. Often, it's the personal myths and storylines we've invented with our egos that have held us back in the past. These are those "middle-sized stories" mythologist Joseph Campbell cautions us to avoid creating. It's not that these limitations haven't really existed; they probably have. But the *way* we perceive them, hold on to them, and build them into dramas or lopsided views is usually at the root of our suffering. Our potential for using our minds to create myths that are life-giving is protection against our own demise.

Your Higher Mind is the Principle, or archetype, that all human thought is organized around. It is the blueprint for perfect reason, for a wholistic outlook in every situation—the bird's-eye view. Your Observer Self is an expression of our Higher Power's Mind. It notices and reminds us that we've taken a wrong turn. Your Higher Mind observes every situation with the keen eye of pure reason. *But this is not an intellectual function; Observer Self is a felt awareness—experienced as "a Moment of Truth."* It is those few seconds of direct inner knowing that come from out of the blue. It awakens you, then moves back and lets your conscious Self decide what your next right action is.

This is how the Observer Self transforms your life—through simple moment-by-moment action, teaching you gently to take responsibility for your life. Without it we could never evolve beyond the definition of a wounded ego. This faithful inner Helper is the key to your Self-realization.

The important thing to remember, though, is not to use this more spiritual view to see how high you can be, but to see integration in it all. Wholeness encompasses both our light side and our darker side. Through aligning your little will with this Divine Intelligence, you'll learn to truly accept it all as having a sacred Purpose for your life. Our personal will then becomes "the will-to-good" and we are harmless to others, for now we revere all life.

Our Higher Mind is the unswerving Will of God coming into form through us. Your ego can misdirect you toward addictive or dysfunctional ways of thinking, feeling, or behaving. You experience this when you are caught in an emotional reaction, motivated by some unmet need.

If you are willing, stop a moment and reflect on a time when you've let an emotional reactivity or extreme bias run ahead of your intelligence and you said or did something that was harmful to someone. Here's a guided imagery that will help:

A GUIDED IMAGERY
TO RELEASE AN EMOTIONAL ATTACHMENT

Find a quiet place to be still for a while, and put yourself into a meditative state: Close your eyes and breathe quietly for a few minutes, simply watching your breath move slowly in and out—saying to yourself "rising, falling, rising, falling" with each breath, until you feel serene. You can put on some calming, meditative music if this helps you go into a light trance.

Feel yourself leaving regular time and entering into a timeless state, a sacred place. . . . Using your creative imagination, see yourself in your mind's eye involved in the particular condition you wish to release. See as vividly as you can a scene where this drama is playing out, and focus intently on it for several seconds, involving yourself completely in it. . . . Feel the feelings that accompany this experience . . . all the way through. . . . *Really involve yourself!* . . . (TAKE A LONG PAUSE.)

And now, see yourself pulling up and out of this created scenario. Lift up, as though you are rising above it. . . . (TAKE A LONG PAUSE.) Once you are completely up and out, look back down at what you've left. See the scene unfolding through the eyes of your Observer Self. See your pain, your actions, your desires. See what is motivating you. . . . (TAKE A LONG PAUSE.)

See the "other" in the scene, and see that person's intentions and actions. See the whole situation all at once. Feel *intuitively* its nature and its purpose. And just allow this awareness to slowly penetrate your mind and heart. . . . (TAKE A LONG PAUSE.)

Send light and love to all who are in the scene. Feel this light and love penetrate everyone there until the whole thing dissolves in a flash of light. . . . (TAKE A LONG PAUSE.) Make this light and love become a felt experience; stay with this until this happens in your consciousness. . . .

Now, just allow it all to dissolve. . . . Feel it disappear as it slowly settles into your consciousness. . . . When the energy has dissipated gradually, bring yourself back by slowly opening your eyes and becoming aware of your body, the room around you, and how you are feeling. . . . (TAKE A LONG PAUSE.)

Take some time to slowly integrate this experience. Reflect on your emotions when you were "down there" and all caught up in your predicament. Name these feelings. Then, recall how you felt when you were "up there," unattached to the details and viewing it from a larger perspective. Now, name these feelings.

Upon completing this experiment, you may be surprised to note that it is the detached, impersonal Self who is the most loving—not the Self who is so personally and intimately involved! Yet we've been trained to believe the opposite.

You may want to meditate, reflect, draw an image or symbol that came to you, or write in your journal for a while to make this experience fully conscious.

Be honest with yourself, and see if you can get hold of the pattern. What set you off? What need caused you to become so intense? What was your mind telling you that made you react in this manner? Herein will lie your attachment, the complex you may be trapped in. Where might you be stuck in your development? Reflect on all this for a while through the eyes of Higher Mind.

On a higher spiritual level, these same urges that compelled you to overreact emotionally are transmuted into compassion for others, and integrating them enables you to wield spiritual force with caution, love, and understanding. Try not to blame yourself if you've made emotional mistakes. For our transformation to occur, the fires of crisis must burn hot—that is why crises are life-altering experiences and pain is our greatest teacher.

The commitment to own our emotional wounds and one-sided views unites us with spiritual purpose. Our personal passions become compassionate service as we grow in maturity and learn to balance our intense emotions. We don't want to relinquish our passionate nature in favor of lukewarm living. This would make life very uninteresting. But, as one of my Guides remarked, "May the earnestness of all those egos become the joy of our one Soul!"

You can probably recall a time when a dream image or symbol materialized in your outer life. Those chance occurrences, when a symbol and your outer life seem to have exactly the same meaning, are what we call *synchronicity*. Synchronicity appears most often when our lives are highly charged with a sense of destiny, when something archetypal is at work.

In our psychological life, we are always trying to reconcile some polarity, constantly needing to discriminate between right and wrong choices. We also know that we can be judgmental and fail to see the good in both sides of anything or anyone, denying the side we judge as negative.

Since we're programmed biologically and emotionally by a doubling process, duality resides at the core of our nature as human beings. Two-ness actually is a foundation block for our growth. We can learn to live within this tension of opposites, like a world-class surfer on a wave, co-creating an ever-possible new and higher thing that integrates both sides in a complementary fashion. From the winged bird's view where Oneness outshines all this duality, we can see that our consciousness is creative.

We have a powerful role in our evolution. Not all of it, individually, of course. It takes all of us together to make up our world. But we are responsible for our part. Therefore, we must take seriously these three facts:

- our thoughts are creative.
- we are life's one and only meaning-makers.
- dualism is part of our design and must be acknowledged, worked through, and accepted before it can be transcended.

This means outer circumstances may not really be your problem or even need to change that much. But how you label all this content, assign it meaning, and interact with it creates what you call your life. Your Observer sees all your reactivity as your silent inner witness and reminds you, with no stake in the outcome, when you are becoming lost or out of balance because of some emotionally laden circumstance.

This Fair Witness consciousness shows you the whole scene through a broader lens. Behind all this confusion it gently points out what is really going on. This helps us see the situation through compassion. On an archetypal level, Observer Self is your Principle of Truth.

The Western Nigerian medicine men called this power of Inner Truth the god, Fa, who lives in the Beyond, or in the transcendent world that exists beyond our ego-created reality. In the belief of these medicine men, each of us has an invisible soul, or Life Principle. And anyone who wishes to know Oneself while living this transitory life must go inward to connect with Fa, the only link to the Beyond. As the Principle of Truth itself, this god is our Observer Self—the only Source who can reveal the true greatness of life.

Often, when we're having great difficulty letting go of an outworn or destructive pattern, the Observer will walk us through it one step at a time while we're wide awake and *acutely* aware of what we're doing. The Self will give us a vignette in vivid color, so we can see our pattern mirrored back. This can be very uncomfortable, but it is often necessary for our healing. When we can get a breath of fresh thought in between all of our action and reaction, we can change our behavior on the spot.

Sometimes, we can even see our predicament with humor. This means a healing is in progress; we're getting unattached. You might have an insight like, "Gradually now, some balance is restored so I can get over my reactivity and face the reality before me. Then, I'll see that a great lesson is being enacted, just for my benefit." Once we've seen something consciously, we can never be unconscious of it again. We may choose to *feign* unconsciousness (and sometimes do), but now we'll know better. What an ingenious, loving Knower we have built right into us!

Once we uncover our major patterns and integrate any loose ends still holding us prisoners of fear, judgment, doubt, or misunderstanding, we are free. And we begin to live in the present with the joy of being fully awake and consciously participating in our own creation story as a *felt experience*.

WE'RE ALL PLAYERS IN THIS DIVINE WORLD DRAMA— BUT WHO'S THE PLAYWRIGHT?

Like a staged play, your life is being acted out while you learn to be loving and true to your highest nature. You may not realize it, but we all create storylines based on how we see ourselves and how we interpret each experience. Once we create our story, we live it out as though it were the Truth. Every participator in our drama then plays out a role exactly as we've defined it! This reality picture is what you are creating from that big world of possibilities. Watch and see!

When we become trapped in some old, limited storyline that no longer serves us, we begin to suffocate and so do our relationships. We can get so entangled in our plots, we forget our greater purpose. When we can feel our connection to God or a Higher Power, we are fulfilled. Jung describes this fulfillment:*

If one knows that one has been singled out by divine choice and intention from the beginning of the world, then one feels lifted beyond the transitoriness and meaninglessness of ordinary human existence, and transported to a new state of dignity and importance, like one who has a part in the divine world drama.

*Carl Jung, *Collected Works* Vol. 11, rev. ed., ed. Gerhard Alder et al., trans. R. Hull (Princeton, N.J.: Princeton University, 1969).

Your role, then, in this divine world scheme is to be willing to be fully your Self. We humans are the only species in all the kingdoms of nature who can *make meaning and feel compassion for the whole.*

Our consciousness, as you can now see, works like a searchlight. We sense something in the spiritual world, feel inspired, and bring it to this world, giving it a name. It can be an idea, a product, a relationship, a dream, a talent, a hope—whatever. We are materializing spirit. Conversely, we can see something in this world through our spiritual perspective. When we do this, we are spiritualizing matter. In other words, when we can give something in our mundane lives significant meaning or sacred Purpose, we have spiritualized it. *This is how we spiritualize the material world—step by step, event by event.*

While we are living this way, we begin to grow more enlightened. As we begin to see the God-self in others, we spiritualize *them*. And they do the same for us. We all learn to acknowledge and empower one another for our true talents, visions, and dreams. We start to shine, and as we become more comfortable with ourselves, we encourage others to shine as well.

Though we learn to become more connected to others, we are constantly guided from *within* by the inner Knower. We let more and more of our true selves show. Whenever we slip below this level of consciousness and function automatically or in our old ways, our Observer prompts us.

Later on, when we are all more enlightened, we'll begin to *materialize as Spirit;* we'll walk this earth as the One who lives from view of the winged bird. We'll be following the path of the Christ, the Buddha, or whoever models Authenticity for us. We will be part of implementing a Divine Plan as courageous co-creators.

To *consciously* choose to become a fully realized being means you are volunteering to be used by the forces of evolution. Instead of just letting nature take its course, individuating you gradually, you will enter onto an accelerated path. And you will transform *by leaps and bounds* through rapid sequences of death and rebirth. Does this sound familiar? Stop and think a minute about your own growth pattern over the past few years.

Now, stop a minute and quickly take stock of your life. Think about the quality of your current relationships and circumstances. How are you seen by your intimates concerning

1. your mental equanimity?
2. your emotional maturity?
3. your need to be in control?

What is the quality of your primary relationship? It is here, within the domain of intimacy that we most often are shown our deepest wounds and our most imbedded attachments or addictions. Be honest. No one is listening but you. Perhaps your Higher Mind has an objective comment to make on your behalf at this point.

If you have a major leftover issue still floating around unhealed, you may need to take some time out, find a therapist or spiritual guide, and go deeply into yourself for a while. Your time of completion may have come. Your identity may be ready to shift into someone more expanded from who you've always thought you were.

The Divine Law of Redemption

Concepts like *redemption* and *salvation* were never intended to be interpreted morally; these are "psychic functions," meaning they interact with your subjective psychological life and produce a *felt* change. To redeem something means to go back, take another look, and heal it through the eyes of understanding. It's not about being good or bad; it's about realigning ourselves with our true intention whenever we've gotten off the mark.

When we are undergoing a transformation, we will encounter the workings of the Divine Law of Redemption. We have an urge to complete any unfinished business within our personal subconscious, any unresolved issues and wounds where we have repressed or denied our real feelings or true nature. Your Observer Self will pick up on this compelling urge; it will point out to you whenever one of your issues surfaces. It will guide you to the help you need.

Redemption is accomplished by recognizing and integrating your unconscious aspects. But healing is a process, not an event; so it will not happen overnight. Therefore, the first part of your process is to *descend* back through your past. The Law of Redemption takes us back through memory lane to retrieve lost and valuable pieces of our lives.

From the winged bird's vantage point and your sense of compassion, you'll be able to look back and feel what it is you must release, or retrieve and integrate. This is true and practical spiritual work.

From your transcendent point of view you'll note that you've been trapped in some illusion. Maybe you are hooked by an unmet need. This is a time to check out every motive, especially for things that are taking a lot of your energy or time.

Without the Higher Mind that remains wholistic and keeps our archetypal perspective, you can get trapped in Humanity's conditions. For this reason, shamans do soul retrieval work and spiritual psychologists work with the process of redemption.

This process of redeeming our wounded or unintegrated fragments enables us to establish in Truth that which could have been lost through misinterpretation. Truth is that tiny mustard seed within every experience that is planted into our consciousness and grows into something substantial, some quality we carry forward from each experience that is real and useful for Humanity. For example, perhaps you are a social worker specializing in child abuse. You become highly esteemed in your community. You even receive a public award. What happens if the job ends? You are forgotten? The medal rusts? The form side of experience fades. What lives on is the essence, the quality of courage, compassion, or service you gave, from not only doing a good job, but from facing your own unresolved issues placed in front of you daily as you worked with clients. You were changed. And your soul can now use these qualities for the sake of the whole.

Your Observer Self is the tamer of your shadow side, the dark, unloved, and un*lived* part of your nature. Your shadow is a conglomeration of the traits you deplore and prefer to notice in others, but never, of course, in yourself. Because parts of your psyche were damaged or didn't mature, you may be ashamed of them. So your psyche built up defense mechanisms that have kept you away from knowing these unwanted aspects of your nature. You've disowned these traits. But this doesn't mean these forbidden traits disappear. They grow stronger when denied—buried in closets of repression in your subconscious mind. This shadowy side of your nature—usually a form of aggressiveness, meanness, or forbidden sexual fascination—hides out just below the surface of your awareness, except on those occasions when it bursts out in an out-of-control overreaction and embarrasses you. The more denial, the stronger its force. As though in a pressure cooker, your shadow churns with all those pent-up feelings you're denying or too ashamed to explore in the light of day. But to be rounded out, we must make our shadow and all the fear and rejection associated with it conscious or we'll be at its mercy forever.

To heal, the shadow has to be exposed and accepted for exactly who and what it is. Then, paradoxically, it won't need to act out so dramatically, though it may still tug at you from time to time. It will always be your dark side.

Your shadow is only the *antithesis* side of the creative process—the "sparring partner" who makes your life exciting. It forces you to weed out anything wrong with your design and to look at what you're trying to ignore. Its sacred function is to force you to work through your dark side, so its energy can be released in appropriate ways. Then, it blesses us with its spiritual gift: it releases your *élan vital*. Your shadow represents some of your passions that have been ill-placed or possibly repressed completely.

Coming to terms with our shadow is very much like managing and loving a hyperactive child. We learn to express our true feelings in safe settings, see them operate, forgive ourselves and others, and learn to accept it all, over and over . . . until all our energies are balanced and can be used for good. This is integration.

When you feel yourself moving toward an overreaction, call out your Observer Self to watch you consciously! You can either do this symbolically in your mind, or you can act it out in the outer world. But be careful about the choice of acting out your shadow; it can cause you more problems. If you just can't stop yourself from acting out, then you need a lesson.

In shadow work, we can learn to have an ongoing dialogue with the differing voices of the shadow, along with all the taunting images that challenge us when we're trying to stop a destructive habit. By clarifying our images and our energies, we will eventually integrate our shadow Self enough so it will no longer threaten us.

At times you may need an objective other such as a therapist or a friend who can help you. It's pretty difficult to see beyond yourself. It is impossible, as the saying goes, to "pull ourselves out of the swamp by our own pigtail."

One night as I was dozing in that place between waking and sleep, my Observer Self kicked in and said, "Look. A very old friend is here for a visit." Then I saw someone with my inner eye that looked very familiar. She was all decked out as your classic southern belle, with billowy hat, flowing ribbons, and all. And very inappropriately, she was out in the middle of a lake all by herself trying to row a boat, standing up and wobbling all around in the choppy water. I wanted to smile and cry at the same time. I could see so plainly her vulnerability and ludicrous helplessness for one so bright. I realized she was an aspect of me I'd been living with for as long as I could remember. My heart melted and I wanted to reach out to her.

I heard myself say, "Well, hello there, dear little Sally. I recognize you. You've lived in me, my mom, and all my aunts. I see you with all your funny, coquettish ways. And I think I love you—because quite frankly, I admire your spunk!" In my dream, I saw the two of us merge. I took off that silly hat, rolled up my sleeves, sat down in the boat, and rowed to the other shore.

My shadow has become my friend. I know her now as the undeveloped, shadowy side of my nature. Consciousness is light; it is the energy of Love. Something is about to show itself so it can be faced, and thereby healed.

∽

Hitting Bottom Is a Sacred Function

Hitting bottom is a stage on this journey we must all face, and it happens in a cyclic fashion. Let's dismantle the illusions around this theme, which is so dreaded and feared. Hitting bottom is the shift we make from being *involved* in a condition to *evolving* right back out of it. The process of identification and dis-identification contains a turning point.

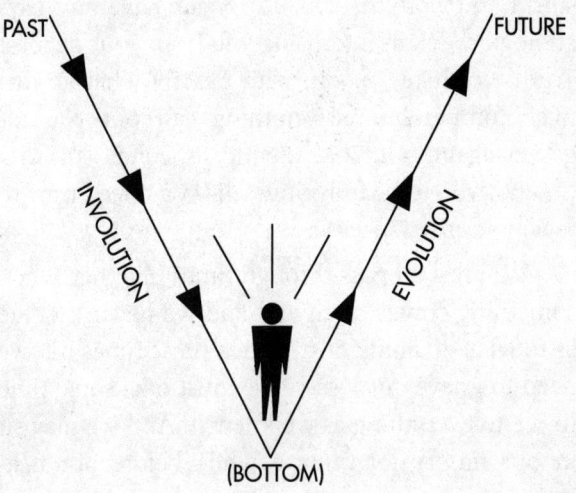

Though hitting bottom feels awful, it has a sacred Purpose which can be seen from "above the storm." At bottom, you no longer have any psychological defenses keeping you from your deepest Truth. So there you sit, with exactly what is. Just like Humpty-Dumpty, nothing can put you together again. Your old identity is gone. This is a time for you to be fully yourself—you need time to regain your perspective.

We must all pass through times like this, when something comes to an end and we haven't a clue as to what's coming next. When these times hit, we need to grieve our losses. We must take some time to die to everything as we knew it. And we may sit in our misery for quite a while before our next right step comes into view.

In our work, we call this "hanging in the dangle." We all hate this stage. Even our keen Observing Mind seems to vanish at times like these; we can't seem to find the bigger picture. We must accept our helplessness and ambiguity for now, feeling pulled this way and that, cry our tears, wail out our rage. We must deal honestly with whatever feelings we have—until the cosmic clock comes 'round and brings us our new life. Rebirth is always just around the corner from bottom.

We need to keep returning to our higher identity, the One at the top, anytime we start getting hooked back into an old pattern. We may swing back and forth for a while like a pendulum, bouncing between attachment and nonattachment, between our old and our wobbly new identity. Sometimes it might feel like you're regressing instead of moving forward. This isn't an easy time for anyone. Time to dis-identify and move on to your next destination. Let go, look to your Higher Self for help, and your evolution will guide you up and out. From bottom Higher Mind shows you a glimpse of the bigger picture. You'll find something to believe in again, and once more, life will seem worthwhile. Some new ideal, some new goal will take shape. New people will start coming into your life. And off you can go toward another dream.

Now that you're waking up, the process of Self-remembrance will become a way of life. Recognized and invited, the observing, nonattached Higher Mind will move into the forefront of your thoughts when you are "asleep at the wheel" and about to make some grave mistake. Observer Self will refocus your attention back to the Truth of any situation.

Here is an example: You're in the midst of reprimanding your teenaged daughter, righteously upholding a long-established family rule. You are even bordering on emotional abuse as your voice rises and you begin to pontificate. Suddenly, Observer nudges you: "Remember, your daughter is individuating—looking for a reason to leave home. Something larger is at stake here." And instantly, through this deeper awareness, you'll be brought out of your robotish stance long enough to take a breath and see the whole picture: Your mother always made you do it, so, as though on automatic, you are treating your daughter the same way. What nonsense, you'll realize. So outdated! Yesterday's "grit" had clouded your view.

Now awake, you can speak to your daughter more gently from your heart. You can still tell her your Truth, but without the pompous intensity. Heart to heart, we can hear one another.

AWARENESS TRAINING

You can begin this practice by saying, "I am aware . . ." at least three times a day. And then consciously observe everything you do and are—your activities, thoughts, feelings, needs. At first, it will only take a minute or two, but don't be discouraged. It's also quite humbling at first, for you will see just how asleep you truly are!

You might want to stop reading and practice being aware for a few minutes. First, note what your body is doing right now. . . . Then your emotions. How are you feeling in your gut? Now, take a minute to watch our thoughts and observe the workings of your brain. You'll get to a place where you'll see that you're not your body, you're not your feelings, nor are you the contents of your mind. You are that higher One who watches it all.

Here's a warning: At times you'll notice static in the communication between you and Observer. Another voice in your head will interfere, criticizing or shaming you for the error you just made. Your ego's inner critic has intruded. You will recognize this voice by its intensity and harsh tone. It is invested in an outcome, whereas Observer never is.

When this happens, go higher and observe that you're in a reactive state and this is some grit from your past. This voice is part of your wounded ego in need of healing. Try to discover why this voice is in your head now. Is it serving some function? If so, try to understand its function. If it's not serving a function, then it's just an old habit you're ready to release.

From Higher Mind's wider spectrum we'll begin to see clearly how some processes and people hook us while other situations seem to just flow on by. What is activated when we are feeling reactive? What did the situation call for? What was it they said? When exactly did you start feeling intense? Was this a familiar feeling? What is the common denominator that always comes up in situations like this? What is it that is even making a scene like this part of your reality? The answers to these questions will show you what is required to become centered in your Self.

An unhealed complex is activated when a current situation or person reminds you of an old hurt, something you've not made conscious. If it's a Mother complex, for example, this means you are still not fully individuated from her, and so her feelings are yours. If she disapproves of you, then *you* disapprove of you! Observing consciously shakes these patterns loose so they can heal.

Here's a quick imagery exercise that will help you disengage from any unhealed authority issues:

Picture yourself stepping out of an image of your mother (or father, or whomever). Use your imagination, and really see this happening. Do this over and over, until the inner image becomes clear. Watch how you behave when you are apart from your parent and free.

Holding on to anger toward another who has hurt you takes a lot of energy. You have to shut down other, more positive parts of yourself in order to stay focused on these old resentments. It's best to release them—for your own mental health.

"But!" you say, "this person really did abuse me. She does not deserve to be forgiven. She is truly mean." This way of thinking contains an error: Forgiving people never releases them from their own karmic balancing. This is between them and their Maker. Forgiving is a matter of freeing up your own energy, which is designed for greater things. Your forgiveness is for you.

Once you know who you are, everyone is seen for who they are and appreciated for their part in this divine world drama, mistakes and all. Sometimes our enemies are our greatest teachers.

Any time you are *feeling* something from its highest, most sacred point in consciousness while simultaneously *knowing* the meaning of it, you are for that moment enraptured. You've stepped into the Beyond, the place Jung called the *unus mundus* (One World) behind all apparent worlds. Intensely felt archetypal experiences bring us total fulfillment. For that moment, we are whole.

Your Higher Mind will eventually bring you a direct experience of the Divine that will remove all doubt that you are more than what you look like and there is indeed a greater world. That is what Jung was referring to when asked if he believed in God. He replied, "No, I don't *believe* in God; I *know* God." These powerful transpersonal experiences not only gratify our deepest longings; they heal the psyche. And they begin to happen often once we befriend our Higher Mind. When we've faced it all, owned it all, and let go of our illusions about how things ought to be, we can relax and enjoy the ride.

Once Observer Self becomes your constant conscious companion, you'll be aware that your self-image is changing and expanding. You'll see that *how* you observe a thing determines the *what* of it. And modern physics knows this now, having finally caught up with what the mystics from every age have always known:

We are never born and we never die;
for we are consciousness itself.

Your Bigger Story

In your Higher Mind, your personal storyline is spread out over a much greater time line than your current "biography." Remember, you have archetypal significance too! Let's go higher now and view you from even a wider lens, from the World of Meaning. The memories of our One Soul, Humanity, are stored here in this higher world.

If you're willing, take a few deep breaths, and let your consciousness move into a timeless, sacred space. And then, listen:

You came into a preselected family for the sacred Purpose of incarnation and to heal this particular part of Humanity. You inherit traits and weaknesses of your predecessors, then make them conscious and heal—or learn from them whatever your soul intends. Your genes are encoded with certain strengths, talents, and distortions that are to be released, expressed, erased, integrated, or transformed. You do this by taking on all that you inherited and becoming conscious. You make spiritually based choices that resolve or correct the problems you carry and represent. Humanity can only be healed by our *assimilation* and *transmutation* of the human condition itself.

In this incarnation we are here to heal this world and evolve it to its next level. This is your sacred Purpose for being on this planet. You are the rescue mission! This is the function of our species. This is our part. And it has always been so. No one can do this for us.

The first part of your life, then, was lived for the sake of your ego's development and its adjustment to the culture in which you were born. Your ego lives right on the surface, the face consciousness wears when it looks out at the world it is to inhabit. In psychology, the ego is referred to as a *persona*, which in Greek means "mask." The ego is our executor who figures out how to live in the outer world by watching others and mimicking society's current ideals. It picks up its cues from society's reward system. Remember when you were small? You wanted to be a good little boy or girl so you could have the ice-cream cone.

From the time we are born, we are being initiated into an outer reality, a culture that demands certain values and standards. So at first, by cosmic law, we are naturally preoccupied with getting our own needs met and with learning to form relationships and activities that will bring us growth.

This first stage of your awakening as a little human being may have been quite an ordeal, however. Flaws are built in right from the start. None of us had completely enlightened parents! This is simply a fact of life. Nor have we been all that wise in parenting our own children—or ourselves, for that matter. Inside your head live two voices, the voice of your ego and the voice of your Higher Self.

Therefore, you must learn to discriminate between these two voices. This daily practice your

Observer Self performs requires a lot of inner work from you. The conflicts that arise from being unaware of the difference produce crises, which are your life's lessons. The word *crisis* is from the Greek word *krinein,* which means "to discriminate or decide." In Chinese, it means "dangerous opportunity." A crisis will burn hot enough to open us up completely. Then, we can see from our larger Reality.

You were born enlightened. You've always been aware of your true origins. But once you were physically embodied, you forgot. It isn't possible to remember the cosmic roots for long, and this is for a cosmic reason: We had to go into an unconscious state to fully take on our human conditions.

Sometimes very small children will shock you with their uncanny understanding of who they really are. I'm reminded here of a precious story I recently heard:

A four-year-old girl greeted her new baby brother when he came home from the hospital and ordered her parents to leave the room while she spoke to him alone. The parents had some anxiety about this, because young children often resent newborns and want to harm them. So the parents ignored this suggestion, to which their daughter stomped her foot and demanded they leave! They stepped outside the door, keeping watch, and saw the sister bend over the crib saying to the baby, "Well, John, I'm glad you're finally here. And listen! You must tell me quickly before you forget: What is God like? I must know, 'cause I've nearly forgotten!"

The rules here were divined by our Higher Power, and were modeled by the Christ, the Buddha, Lord

Shiva, Shakti, and other Divine Beings who have come here as our enlightened Masters. Here is the dominant rule they each lovingly modeled for us:

We are to take it all on fully. And dance our way through life's experiences, both the joys and all the sorrows. And then, and only then, can we dis-identify and rise "up and out."

It is written in your "job description" that at some point you must have the courage to come out and be your Self as our great Teacher has done. No more cop-outs, no more games. No more superficial living. No more hiding from each other or from ourselves. This world is starving for authenticity, so You are it!

You model this awakening by simply evidencing the *faith* you have in the process, based on your own experience. You are a vision carrier, a light bearer for this world. This is all there is to it—it is such a simple task, yet so very removed from how we've all been programmed.

If you are like me, leaping and bounding through constant change, you probably could use a little supportive companionship along the way. Self-understanding provides a great cushion for this experience. The company of others of like mind and intention are often our salvation. For here, in the fast lane, your world is rarefied. Most people get stuck along the way in the ego's world of outer focus, and it gets lonely! It's important to stay close to those who are awakening with you.

Once you commit to this way of living, you are in for a thrilling surprise: Your real kin will start to surface all around you when your awareness of this greater life is soundly established. When you meet one you've a deep soul connection to, you feel an instant recognition. You will share a quiet knowing that you truly understand each other—a deep, abiding, nonattached love.

These are your soul brothers and sisters, here to involve in your true destiny. These are very ancient ties, yet newly discovered—like the return of a future memory. Through these deep connections your life will become empowered with Spirit.

And, like the pieces in a cosmic puzzle, we will each eventually find our correct fit. Then, we'll be *in* Right Relationship. Ego and Essence (soul),

Mind and Heart, masculine and feminine, God and Humanity, brother and sister, will have all become One.

"And Help Me to Do My Part"

In true Love there is no carpet to sweep anything under. Everything is seen, felt, and acknowledged. Each one of us must take full responsibility for our part. No one else can do your part for you. Our problems are not just personal; and neither is our healing or creative expression only for ourselves: Anytime we heal a condition in our personal lives or create some new inspired response, a little more light shines brightly on our One Humanity. . . . A little more of the real Self stands revealed.

Without the aid of our bird's-eye view, we would truly be lost in the maze of human fragmentation. With deep gratitude we can honor our inner Knower, our Higher Mind, for giving us the view that can contain all of who we are. This archetypal Self will always remind us of both our human frailties and our immortal divinity.

We can learn to be "above the storm," as Higher Mind, and know that all our experiences, even the painful ones, have a sacred Purpose. And we can lovingly, even joyously, accept our plight. We forgive ourselves and one another for the mistaken notions and wrong turns we've made that became our instruments for transformation. From the silence of our one Heart, we can understand what the great Indian sage, Sri Aurobindo, meant when he told his disciple,

By thy stumblings, this world is perfected.

∞